Mr. Jim's
Magical
Secrets

Illustrated by the author

SPS Publications

Also by James L. Merrills
Magicians in the Making: A Complete Guide to Hosting a Magic Camp

APPRECIATION

Words can not express my gratitude to David R. Goodsell (former President of the Society of American Magicans and director of the West Coast Wizard's Magic Camp). His generosity and touch of "magic" has influenced nearly every facet of my magic career — including Kristi and Sara's love for magic, our mid-West "Magic Camps," and some of the most wonderful opportunities of my professional life of magic. Thank you, David.

Magical Secrets
Second Edition
By James L. Merrills, Prestidigitator
© 1999; 2003 by James Merrills, all rights reserved.

Experience the Magic
James L. Merrills
12916 Brody
Marcellus, Michigan 49067
Web Site: www.mr-jim.com
Email: magic@mr-jim.com

About the Authors

Mr. Jim Merrills has enjoyed magic since childhood. Through Experience the Magic (www.mr-jim.com), he has presented prevention programs to over a million students across the nation. His programs focus on drug and violence prevention, physical education (like juggling and cup stacking), and more.

Mr. Jim served as an instructor for the former West Coast Wizard's Magic Camp (California), after developing his own magic camps in the mid-West. Magic camps teach basic presentation skills, which result in increased personal confidence and leadership abilities.

Miss Kristi (age 16), a junior magician, began her career in magic at age seven, attending the West Coast Wizard's Magic Camp for six years. She gained the attention of Milton Bradley's Magic Works staff for the design of her "Impossible Sword Box," and sold the same to magicians across North America. She loves performing the dancing cane and juggling.

Miss Sara (age 12) has been the "opening performer" for many magic shows, and assists with school, library and community presentations. She enjoys performing magical productions and teaching other students about the sport of cup stacking.

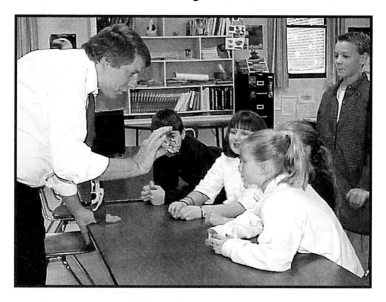

The author teaching junior magicians.

CONTENTS

INTRODUCTION

Purchasing this book was a wise decision, for many reasons. First, reading is great! You can learn a lot by reading. I do not know of any good magician who does not possess his or her own library of magic books. Second, you can take this book with you anywhere you go! This means that you can read, review and practice anytime. And "practice" is one of the foremost rules for a good magician.

This book contains a number of the tricks taught in our magic camps. Many magic tricks are visual puzzles; if you know how the "pieces" fit together, then you understand how the trick is done. But the word magic suggests more than just a trick. It implies that a person has the ability to create wonder or excitement. Consequently, those who expose magic secrets are demonstrating that they misunderstand what the art of magic actually is.

There are many types of magic: productions, vanishes, transformations, levitations, penetrations and restorations. All of them can create a sense of awe, because they appear to defy natural laws. You will find a variety of these in this book.

Among the tricks in this book, you will find suggestions on presentation, misdirection, and patter (the words you use), in the hope that your magic is as entertaining as possible. My goal is to assist you in becoming a good "junior magician." Remember, every great magician started small, and you do not know what the future may hold for you. But you can begin now to shape the future. Good luck, young Magish!

RULES OF MAGIC
A good magician...

Never reveals the secret!

Revealing a secret destroys the wonder and enjoyment. Anyone can do a trick. Only a magician can cause a trick to come to life, creating magic.

Never performs the same trick twice!

You can only surprise your spectator once. Repeating a trick never surprises the spectator twice, and often allows him to figure out the secret.

Never performs a trick without practice!

Practice the trick and what you will say (the "patter"). Practicing in front of a mirror will show you the spectator's view. The patter can make a trick more entertaining, or provide needed misdirection; an audience may miss your most obvious actions because they are concentrating on your words.

Remember, your goal is to entertain, not just "trick." If the audience enjoys your magic, they will look forward to seeing more it.

PART 1 - MAGIC

THE GIRLS' FAVORITE

Materials
Rubber band or girl's hair tie
Trick
A rubber band mysteriously jumps between the fingers.

This trick was so-named because some girls have used round elastic hair ties, instead of rubber bands, to perform this trick.

Place an elastic band around both your first (index) and middle fingers of your right hand, with your palm facing you, and your fingers pointing upwards. Slide your left hand's first finger down inside the band, along the back side of your right fingers. Stretch the band away from your right fingers, then to the left, then to your right, and then toward yourself and to the left, going over your right thumb.

With the band stretched to the left (in front of your palm) quickly insert the right four finger tips down inside the rubber band's loop. Lift out your left finger, allowing the band to lie against the right fingernails. (From the spectator's view, the rubber band is only around the first and middle fingers.) As you quickly flip the right fingers up, the band will quickly jump to the ring and little fingers! Practice this in front of the mirror until you are confident about performing.

[Tip: I slap the back of my right fingers as they flip up. This hides the rubber band's movement.]

RE-CAP

Materials
Plastic Pen with Cap

Trick

A plastic pen cap mysteriously returns to the pen; but only for you!

This is a great impromptu trick, and it is the first trick that Miss Kristi ever performed in front of a school assembly.

Remove the cap from the pen, and hand it to the spectator. Explain that most plastic pen caps have a small magnet embedded in the plastic that can not be seen. This, you explain, helps keep the cap on.

To demonstrate the magnetic property of the cap, hold the pen in the left hand with the ink end aimed up and toward the right hand. Hold the cap in the right hand, with the opening downward, near the pen. Slowly bring them together, keeping the cap slightly higher than the pen.

As they come close together, squeeze the tip of the cap between your right thumb and first finger. The tight squeeze will force the cap to "shoot out" from between the fingers and on to the end of the pen, giving the appearance that magnetism has pulled the cap on. (Experiment with a few different brands of pens to see which type works best for you. I prefer a tapered cap.)

FRENCH DROP

Materials

A coin (quarter or half dollar)

Trick

A coin suddenly disappears from your finger tips!

The French Drop is one of the most popular coin illusions, and a great first coin trick for any beginning magician.

Hold the coin horizontally (like a plate) between your right thumb and your first, second and third fingers, palm facing you. Bring your left fingers over the right fingers as if you are going to take the coin—this action should appear natural. Just as your left fingers make downward contact with the right fingers, pull your right thumb back slightly, allowing the coin to fall in your bowl-shaped palm. (The spectator will not see the coin drop in your palm if your three right fingers are close together.) Curl your left fingers closed, while pulling them away from the right hand, giving the impression that the coin is in the left hand. At the same time, turn the right hand palm down, and let it hang by your side, allowing the coin to rest in your fingers, hidden from sight. (If your left hand remains closed, with your eyes on it, and the right hand relaxed by your side, the spectator will follow your eyes and closed hand.)

Turning your body so your right hand—and coin—are blocked from the spectator's view, ask the spectator to rub the back of your left hand, which is supposedly holding the coin. While their attention is on the left hand, raise the coin to your right pocket, dropping it in, and continue bringing your right hand upward. Pick up your wand (or pencil) and wave it over your left hand. Slowly open your hand, showing that the coin has disappeared.

MYSTERIOUS WRAPPED COIN

Materials
Sheet of Paper and Coin

Trick
A coin disappears, while wrapped securely inside a folded piece of paper.

Prepare by folding a sheet of paper (8.5 x 11) in half, and then in half again. The folded quarters should measure about 4 x 5. Tear or cut out one of the sheet's quarter pieces.

Hold the paper (the long way) left to right. Place the coin against the center of the sheet, while you fold the top portion over it, so the coin is completely covered. (Using patter will distract your spectator from closely observing how you are folding the

Mr. Jim teaching at a famous magic camp in California.

paper.) Next, fold the ride side back and behind the coin. Then fold the left side back and behind the coin. There is still an opening at the bottom—don't let the coin fall out. Finally, fold the bottom portion back, and behind the coin.

(From the spectator's view, you have folded the paper from the top, sides, and bottom, securing the coin inside. But only you know that the last—bottom—fold actually left an opening in the bottom, where the coin can slide out.)

Holding the paper in your left hand, allow the coin to slide out and into your left palm, without anyone seeing. Taking the paper with the right fingers, reach into your pocket with the palmed coin (left hand) to obtain some "magic dust." Drop the coin into the pocket, and pretend to bring something out of the pocket, sprinkling it on the paper, in your right hand. Blow lightly on the paper. Now open it slowly, showing that the coin has vanished!

DISAPPEARING QUARTER IN CUP

Materials

A quarter, paper cup, and scissors

Trick

You place a quarter in a cup and it vanishes!

Prepare the cup by cutting a slit on the side, near the bottom, large enough for the coin to slide through.

Holding the cup, with the slit hidden against the palm, ask a spectator to drop a coin inside. (Have a coin in your pocket, in case he does not have one.) Having them drop the coin in makes the situation appear natural.

When ready, tilt the cup, allowing the quarter to slide out into your palm. Keep the coin hidden

between your palm and the cup. Say, "To some people money is like water. But if that were true we could just toss it back out." As you say the word "toss," jerk your forearm away from you, as if you are tossing the coin out of the cup. The coin will remain trapped between the palm and cup. Your spectator will react with surprise. Quickly put the cup away, not allowing them to inspect the cup or your hand.

THE GROWING COIN
Materials
Nickel and quarter (silver coins)
Trick
A coin grows in size, while hanging in mid-air!

This is a simple, but powerful, coin transformation. With a little practice, you will be able to astonish your spectators.

Reach into your right pocket and palm a quarter (Keep the coin hidden against your palm, held between the fatty skin of the thumb and little finger.) Squeeze the nickel between your thumb and first finger, and curl the other fingers.

Explain how tossing a coin high enough will cause it to disappear! By saying this, the spectator will expect the coin to disappear, misdirecting his attention from your true actions. Gently swing your forearm upward a few times, as if you are preparing to toss the coin. If you look upward, so will the spectator. (Your eyes will misdirect the spectator's eyes from the "real" action.)

On the final upward swing, continue to squeeze the nickel while you toss the palmed quarter into the air. While your eyes follow the silver coin (quarter) upward, you should have time to quickly slip the nickel into your pocket. (Practice this before performing!) Finally, catch the quarter when it comes down, quickly closing the hand around it. Immediately flip the hand over onto the back of your other hand, keeping the coin hidden. Lifting the upper hand say, "It may not have disappeared, but the return on my money is great!"

DISAPPEARING COIN

Materials
Coin, hanky and secret assistant
Trick
After several spectators examine a coin under a cloth, it disappears without a trace!

This is an easy trick with a surprise ending, but you will need a secret assistant. Pick your assistant wisely! Clearly explain to your assistant what will happen, so she understands what is expected of her.

Produce a coin, and let the audience examine it. Hold it between your thumb and first finger, spreading and centering a hanky over it and your hand.

Explain that you are not doing anything "tricky," lifting the cloth and showing the coin again. While sharing your patter, approach a few spectators, asking them to reach under the hanky and touch the coin, insuring that it is still there.

The last person to check the coin is your assistant. Reaching under, she secretly palms the coin, dropping her hand casually. If her actions are smooth and normal, no one will suspect anything sneaky.

Return to your performing area and wave a wand over the hanky. Slowly (with some acting) lift one corner, and remove the cloth from the hand. The coin is gone, and everything can be examined!

PEN PREDICTION

Materials
Capped pen, paper and assistant
Trick
You are able to read someone's mind as you enter a room!

This is a simple prediction trick, which requires an assistant who understands how the trick works.

After you leave the area, your assistant selects a volunteer, asking them to write any number between 1 and 12 on a piece of paper. Your assistant watches, insuring that the directions are followed. The volunteer is asked to fold the paper a number

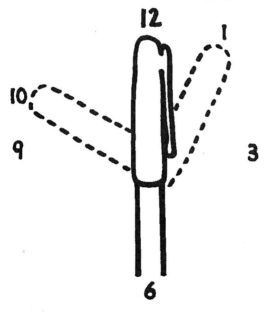

Kristi and Mr. Jim making a rabbit appear.

of times and lay it down with the pen, returning to her seat.

While the assistant (who has seen the number) recaps what has happened for the audience, he picks up the pen, pointing it toward the volunteer. The trick's secret is now found in how the assistant lays the pen down.

When the magician returns (after the assistant leaves or turns away), he will see which direction the capped (or ball) end of the pen is pointing. Like the face of a clock, if the capped end is pointing toward the audience, the chosen number is "12." If it points toward the magician, the number is "6." If to the right, it is "3." To the left is "9."

If you prefer to use fewer numbers, ask the spectator to pick a number from 1 to 4. In this case every quarter turn of the pen increases the value by one.

Note: You could do this trick twice. Instead of using the pen's direction the second time, the placement of the cap's tail on the pen can reveal the number between 1 and 4. Use the lettering on the side of the pen to designate the "1." Turn the cap clockwise, a quarter turn, for the number "2," and so forth.

MY FAVORITE ANI-MULE!

Materials
Index cards (6), pencil or crayons
Trick
You predict which animal a spectator will pick.

Prepare by drawing five different animals (e.g., cat, dog, ferret, bunny, giraffe) on five different cards; one animal per card, on only one side. Draw a mule on the sixth card. Draw a large question mark [?] on the back side of all six cards. Finally, place the cards face-down in a pile, with the mule card fourth from the top. You are ready to begin.

You say, I have pictures of six different animals on these six face-down cards. Now, I will attempt to predict which ani-mule—er—I mean, ani-mal, you will choose." Then ask, "Do you know how to count to six?" They will probably say yes. Then ask, "Do you know how to spell your numbers." Again, they should say, yes. Finally, ask them to call out any number from 1 to 6.

No matter which number they pick, they will always pick the mule! If they say 4, count down to the fourth face-down card. If they say 5, spell "F I V E," from the top down. If they say 3, SPREAD the cards to the right, and count (from the left) to the third card. If they pick 1, 2, or 6, spread the cards to the right, and spell to the card. (One, two and six are all three letter words.

To maintain the suspense, reveal all the other animal pictures first. As you turn over the selected (mule) card say, "You did pick the ani-mule!"

CRAYON PREDICTION

Materials
3 crayons

Trick
You can immediately tell which color someone is thinking of!

Hand a box of crayons to a spectator and ask him to select three completely different colored crayons (e.g., red, green, and black), but not to tell you which ones he picked. Turn away as he does this. Ask him to close the box, so you cannot see which three have been removed. While you are still turned, ask him to place one of the three in your hand, behind your back, and place the other two behind his back.

Momentarily turn toward the spectator, stating that you will "attempt to read his mind." While looking at him, secretly scratch your thumbnail up and down along the tip the crayon, obtaining a little color on top of and underneath the nail. Turning away again, ask the spectator to take the crayon back, and place it behind his back, with the other two.

Finally, turn and face the spectator. Press your index fingers lightly against his temples (the sides of his forehead), and your thumbs against the center of his forehead. Quickly glance at the color on your thumbnail, and then name the selected color while staring deep into his eyes.

E.S.P. PREDICTION

Materials

5 index cards, pen and secret assistant

Trick

You instantly determine which symbol a person is thinking of.

This is a great "mind reading" trick, which will baffle your audience. You will need a secret assistant.

Prepare by drawing the following picture lines on five index cards: a circle (1 line) a cross (2 lines), three wavy lines (3 lines), a square (4 lines) and a five-pointed star (5 lines).

Now, explain to your secret assistant that a spectator will select one E.S.P. (which stands for, Extra Sensory Perception) symbol, by pointing to it while you are out of the room.

Your assistant, and everyone else present, will see which card (symbol) the volunteer points to. Your assistant will now lay the corresponding number of fingers (1-5) along the edge of the table or against her cheek. When you return, you only need to glance at the number of fingers showing or standing out.

For example, if the volunteer picks the cross, the assistant will extend two fingers. Glance at the number of fingers that are extended, and then act as if you are concentrating on the volunteer's thoughts. After a few moments, announce the E.S.P. symbol that they selected.

HOW DO YOU SPELL MAGIC?

Materials

5 index cards and pen

Trick

A spectator picks the correct card by spelling the word magic.

Prepare five index cards by writing "No" on four of them and "You are Magic!" on one. Make a small secret notch in the "Magic" card with your fingernail.

Hand all five cards to the spectator, with the written messages face-down. Ask her to mix the cards. Taking the cards back, ensure that the notched card is second from the top. If not, casually spread the cards while talking, and cut as necessary.

Hand the cards to the spectator, explaining that you would like her to do a little magic. Ask her to spell the word magic, dealing one card to the bottom of the pile for each letter called. The card corresponding to the last letter ("C") should be turned over. The word "No" will come up. Discard it. She is to continue in this manner until there is only one card left in her hand. Turning over the last card, she will see the message, "You are Magic!"

(This could be done with five playing cards. Use four Aces and a Joker, notching the Joker. You can use any five-letter word or phrase, like "Mr. Jim.")

3 COLORED PREDICTION

Materials

3 index cards, paper, manilla envelope, and crayons

Trick

The spectator can read your mind!

Prepare by drawing a large blue dot on one card, a green dot on the second, and pink dot on the third. Next, draw a large blue dot on the back of the envelope, a green dot on the back of all the cards, and a pink dot on a piece of paper. Put the paper and the cards in the envelope.

To begin, remove the three cards from the envelope, face up (green, blue, and pink dots showing), and lay them in front of the spectator. Ask them to concentrate on your thoughts and to state the color you are thinking of. Regardless of their response, say "Very good!"

If they pick blue, put the cards back in the envelope, and turn the envelope over, revealing the blue dot. If they choose green, turn over all the cards, one at a time, revealing all the green dots. If they say pink, pull the paper from the envelope revealing the pink dot. (Put everything away quickly, and move on to your next trick.)

MAGICIAN'S CHOICE

Materials

Paper and pencil

Trick

The spectator selects the correct item!

You have been asked to do some magic, but you do not have any magic props. Ask someone for a sheet of paper and pencil.

Tear off four small pieces of paper. Secretly write the letter "B" on one piece, fold it a few times, and lay it aside. This is your prediction.

Write the letters "A", "B" and "C" on the other three pieces, and show these to your spectator. Ask the spectator to point to any of the three pieces. (They only have two options: they will point to the predicted "B," or one of the other letters.)

If they select the "B," ask them to pick it up. You then pick up the folded piece and open it, revealing your prediction skills.

If they point to "A" or "C", pick it up and crumple it, tossing it aside. Now, ask them to pick up one of the two remaining pieces. (Note: The first time you ask them to point to one of the pieces. The second time you ask them to pick up one of the pieces.)

If they pick up the "B," ask them to hand it to you, and reveal your written prediction. If they pick up the wrong letter, ask them to crumple it, like before. Then open your prediction and lay it by the "B" paper.

MATH-MAGIC PREDICTION

Materials

Paper and Pencil

Trick

You accurately predict a total, before the spectator picks the numbers!

Prepare by secretly writing "1089" on a piece of paper, and folding it.

Explain that you have made a prediction, and that you intend to influence your spectator's choice. Look into her eyes and ask her to name three digits (not "0"). Write them down on a sheet of paper, in the order she says them. Explain that she could have chosen any number, but you influenced her to pick the very digits she named, and in that order!

Write the same numbers in reverse, and subtract the lesser number from the greater. Explain that no one could have known the numbers she would pick, or the final result.

Next, reverse the result. Now add the actual result and the reversed result together. The total will be 1089. Open your prediction upside down, showing the numbers 6801. She will think you failed. Finally, turn the paper over, showing that they match!

SCHOOL BOOK TEST

Materials

2 books

Trick

You can immediately state which words can be found on any page in a book!

Prior to the presentation, open the book that the spectator will be given. Open it near the middle, and remember the page number, the first and last words on the page, and what the page is about.

Ask your volunteer to name one of the books. Using the principle called "magician's choice," hand them the book you prepared.

Begin flipping through the pages of your book, asking them to say "stop." When they do, call out the page number you had read in their book (not the one you are looking at). Ask them to open their book to the same page number, and to concentrate on the first word on the page. Slowly begin to pronounce the word, as if you are getting a mental impression of it. (You could also describe the word.) Next, ask them to focus on the last word on the page, and slowly reveal the word

Finally, describe the content of the page, mentioning a few words on the page. Your spectator will be amazed at your abilities!

LINKING SILVER

Materials
Paper Clips (2) and Dollar Bill
Trick
You instantly link two paperclips together without touching them!

The famous Chinese Linking Rings are one of my favorite magic props. You can perform a similar trick, close up, with a couple paper clips.

Holding a dollar bill between your hands, fold the left third toward yourself, but do not crease it. Fold the right third away from yourself, but do not crease it. (If folded correctly, the bill will stand on its own, and will look like a "Z" from above.)

Looking down on the "Z," clip one end of the bill to the center, then clip the other end to the middle section.

Grasp the ends of the bill and quickly pull them away from each other, with a quick motion. The paper clips will jump into the air, linking together.

PENCIL-BREAKING DOLLAR

Materials
New pencil and dollar bill
Trick
You prove that paper can cut solid wood!

Fold the dollar in half length-wise (the long way). Ask the spectator to hold out his hands, palms up. Lay the ends of the pencil on both palms. There should be a lot of space between his hands. Ask him to curl his fingers over the pencil.

With the crease [v] held downward, hold the bill over the pencil. Now "karate chop" the wood. The paper will only rub against the pencil, with no damage to the bill or pencil.

Attempt this again, asking him to hold the ends tightly. Line the crease [v] with the middle of the pencil. When ready, lift the hand upward, secretly extending your first (index) finger along the length of the bill. As your hand comes down, the finger will hit the center of the pencil first, breaking it in half. Immediately curl your finger back.

The spectator will be amazed, and unable to repeat the performance.

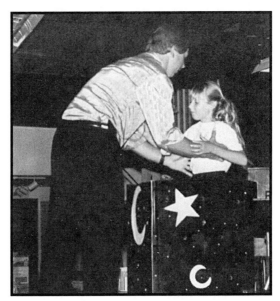

Miss Kristi's Sword Box Illusion.

DOLLAR BILL ESCAPE

Materials

Envelope and dollar bill

Trick

A dollar vanishes from a sealed envelope!

Prepare the envelope by secretly cutting a one-half inch long slit across the middle of the envelope's front side.

Lay the envelope in your hand, with the cut side down. Ask the spectator to fold a dollar bill in half, back side out, four times. (The small size will make it easier to slide the dollar through the slit later.)

Explain that you will mentally determine the serial number on the dollar, without seeing it! As you slide the bill into the envelope, push it through the hole, hiding it between the envelope and your palm. Lick and seal the cover of the envelope, creating the illusion that the bill is secure inside.

Explaining that you need special "x-ray" dust, reach into your pocket, with the dollar secretly palmed. Leave the dollar in the pocket. After you sprinkle the dust on the envelope, attempt to read its contents, touching the corner against your temple. Suddenly, act as if something has gone wrong, and rip the envelope in half. (Tearing it into smaller pieces will destroy the secret.) Finally, admit that you were not able to read the dollar's numbers as it disappeared too quickly.

NOT KNOT?

Materials
Rope (3-foot length)
Trick
You challenge the spectator to tie a knot in a rope. She can not, but you can!

Lay the rope across the table. Ask the spectator to grasp the ends, and tie an overhand knot, without letting go of the ends. She can not do it.

(Be patient, giving her plenty of time to attempt this feat.)

After she gives up, cross your arms. (One hand should be sticking out and the other tucked in, like a pretzel.) Lean over the table and pick up the ends. Pick up the left end with the right hand, and visa-versa. Holding on to the ends, slowly pull your arms apart. A knot will be created near the middle of the rope.

KNOT SO FAST!

Materials

Rope (3-foot length)

Trick

Only you can make the fastest knot in the world.

Prepare the rope by pulling out the core (if it has one). This makes it more flexible. Tie a loose knot about four inches from one end.

When ready, hold one end in each hand, stretching the rope in front of you. The knot should be hidden in your right hand. (The short ends should hang out the side of each hand, appearing natural.)

While speaking, place the left end between your right fingers, and drop your left hand. (Your right hand is now holding both ends with the center portion hanging down.) Turn your right hand palm down and begin rotating the wrist in a circular motion. Explain that you are about to make "the fastest knot in the West!"

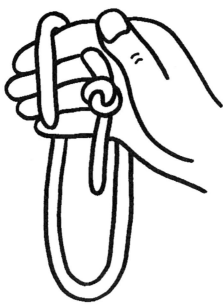

Snap the rope away from your body, opening your finger tips, and releasing the unknotted end. No knot will be seen. "Almost," you say, "I'll try again."

Squeeze the unknotted end between the right fingertips again, and repeat the circular motion with the wrist. This time, open your hand (while squeezing the unknotted end) as you snap your wrist, releasing the knotted end. With the knot hanging there in view, you say "And that is the fastest knot in the West!"

HOUDINI WRIST ESCAPE

Materials

2 ropes (3 feet each)

Trick

You escape, while tied to another person!

Prepare by removing each rope's core.

Begin by tying one rope to the spectator's wrist, one end around each wrist. (Do not tie it too tightly, and do not leave extra rope on the outside of the knots. You want plenty of rope between their wrists.) You now have an unbroken circle, created by the spectator's body, arms, and rope.

Ask the spectator to tie the other rope to your wrists in the same way, with three or four knots on each wrist, ensuring that you can not escape quickly. (Note: he must drape one end of your rope over and through his, before tying your second wrist. In this way, your "circle," and his, are connected together, like two linking rings.) Point out that neither of you could possibly become free without untying the knots.

Ask the spectator to turn his head away to the

right and close his eyes, as you turn your body to your right. (You are now facing opposite directions.)

Quickly grasp the center of your rope with your left hand and place it against the inside of your right forearm, just below your wrist and the tied knot. Slide this middle loop of rope under and up through the circle tied around your right wrist. Pull this loop upward, past your right palm, and over your right hand. Bring the rope down the back of your hand, and continue pulling on it. The ropes will unlink.

Your spectator will be astonished to find that you have escaped so quickly, without untying the knots!

SPOOKY HANKY

Materials
Handkerchief or small cloth.
Trick
A handkerchief mysteriously comes to life!

Hold the center of the cloth with your right fingertips. With the left hand, stroke the material downwards, straightening the material. On the final down stroke, hold the lower half in your closed left hand, with left thumb upright on the backside (nearest you), hidden from the spectator's view.

Explain that you need a hair, and pretend to pluck one from your head, with your right hand. Pretend to thread the hair through the top (tip) of the hanky, with a final "tug" straight up.

Now, with your right hand slightly above the cloth's tip, act as if you are moving the hair forward and back. At the same time, use your left thumb and first finger (which are holding the cloth) to tip the cloth forward and back, in concert with the right hand's movement. Finally, move your right hand directly above the cloth, and hold the cloth up straight. Quickly jerk your right hand upward, acting as if you have snapped the hair. Put the cloth away.

RESTORED NEWSPAPER CLIP

Materials

Newspaper, scissors, rubber cement, baby powder.

Trick

After cutting a strip of newspaper into two pieces, you restore it by magic!

Prepare by cutting a column from a newspaper (about 12-inches long and 2-inches wide). Smear a thin coat of rubber cement over the middle section of the strip, covering about six inches. After the cement dries, sprinkle a light coating of powder over the cemented area. Hold the strip over a garbage can and shake off the excess powder. Lay the strip inside of a newspaper, and gently fold the paper. (This trick is best performed "on stage," rather than close up.)

Pretend to cut a strip out of the newspaper, and lift up the prepared column. Fold it in half (cement on the inside), lining up the edges. The crease should be on top, with ends hanging down. Cut across the column, by the crease. Now, slowly lift one end. It will appear that the strip is restored. (The cutting action causes the glue to stick where the cut was made.)

Fold the strip in half again, and cut the strip at

an angle. When you lift an end, the column will form an angle!

DOG SCENTS

Materials
Any 5 objects (coins, dollars, pencils, etc.) and a secret assistant

Trick
Walking into a room, you immediately know which object someone has selected!

Explain to your assistant how you will point to five objects, naming them by number ("one," "two," and so on) in a straight row. While you are out of the room, the assistant will note which object is selected by the volunteer. When you return, your assistant is to casually hold his hand up to his cheek, as if thinking, extending the number of fingers that match the selected object.

Lay five objects on a table, in front of the spectators. Explain that after you leave the room, one of them should "lightly touch" one object. When you return to the room, quickly note the number of fingers your assistant is showing. Approach the table, and hold your hand over the objects. Move your hand over them slowly. Finally, point to the object that was touched.

3-GLASS CHALLENGE

Materials
3 glasses (or paper cups)

Trick
Only you can turn all three glasses upright, in the required number of moves.

This type of trick is also called a "sucker trick," and is often used in a bet with a friend.

Place three glasses on the table, in a row, with only the center glass mouth up. (The cups must be in this position for the trick to work.) Challenge a friend to (1) turn all three glasses mouth up, (2) in only three moves, (3) turning two glasses with each move.

Demonstrate by doing the following:

Move #1—turn over the left and middle

Move #2—turn over the left and right

Move #3—turn over the middle and left

All the glasses should now be mouth up.

Now, turn only the middle cup mouth down (the wrong starting position!), and challenge the spectator to perform the same routine, finishing with all the cups mouth up. He cannot do it!

6-GLASS CHALLENGE

Materials

6 glasses

Trick

Only you can solve the "6-Glass Challenge!"

This "sucker trick" is a good follow-up to the 3 Glass Challenge.

Lay six glasses in a row. Fill the three on the left with water; leave the three on the right empty. Explain that the spectator can only move one glass, resulting in the following order when finished: full, empty, full, empty, full and empty.

After she admits defeat, pick up the middle glass of water (second from the left). Remind her that she could only move one glass. Hold the glass over the empty glasses, and pour the water into the middle empty glass (second from the right). Place the glass down in its original position, and smile big!

PENETRATING SILK

Materials
Two silk cloths or hankies, a clear plastic glass and rubber band

Trick
A cloth penetrates a glass!

This is a great trick to perform on stage, or in your living room.

Pick up the glass and one of the cloths. (It is best if the cloths are two different colors.) Place the cloth in the glass, and push it down so it bunches up tightly in the bottom. Pick up the second cloth, open it, and shake it gently, showing both sides. Drape it over the glass.

As you drape the cloth, turn the glass over, so it is upside-down. (The cloth inside the glass should remain on the bottom.) Place the rubber band over the draped cloth and around the top (actually the bottom) of the glass. It will appear as though the mouth of the glass is sealed, but it is actually turned down.

Now state that you will cause a solid cloth to pass through solid glass, "removing the cloth through the bottom of the glass." Reach up under the draped cloth, into the upside-down glass, and grasp the bunched cloth. Slowly lower your hand until the cloth comes out of glass, and is in full view. Lay it on the table.

Remove the rubber band from the cloth that is over the glass. As you are removing the cloth, the hand underneath should turn the glass upright. The glass is mouth up, and the spectator is none-the-wiser. Everything can be examined.

PENETRATING QUARTER

Materials
Wristwatch, handkerchief and two quarters
Trick
A coin penetrates through a solid cloth!

This is one of my favorite tricks, and I have performed this hundreds of times.

Prepare by tucking a quarter under your watch's band, on the palm side of your left wrist. Lay the other quarter in view.

Pull out your hanky and show both sides. (Do not expose the quarter under the band!) Turn your left hand so your thumb and first finger are on top, making a small circle with your fingers. Drape the hanky over the left hand, centering it so the sides hang down evenly. Poke the center of the cloth into the hole. Pick up the coin (that the spectator sees) and place it in the hole.

Ask a volunteer to place her first (index) finger inside the hole, touching the coin. Squeeze your left thumb and index finger around her finger. Ask her to pull her finger out slowly, leaving the coin inside. At the same time, bring your right hand under the hanky and secretly remove the coin from under the band, bringing it into view.

Without saying a word, quickly place the quarter back underneath, but slide it under the backside of the watch. (A watch is usually wider than the band, and can hide the coin completely from view.) Again, ask her to place her finger inside your fist, touching the coin. Slowly push the coin upward as you spread the cloth. She will assume that this is the same coin that you pulled from under the cloth.

Pull the cloth off with your right hand, while turning the left hand palm up. (The watch and coin are now out of view.) Grasp another corner with the left fingers and hold the cloth up, showing that there are no holes or extra coins.

BROWN BAG PREDICTION

Materials
Brown lunch bag and old playing cards
Trick
You are able to locate four matching pieces!

[Note: This trick will ruin your cards. Practice with old playing cards or index cards.]

Select about six playing cards. Open the lunch bag and stand it upright on the table. Pick up the first card and tear it in half, and then tear each piece in half. You now have four quarter pieces. Place each piece, one at a time, into the bag. Then do the same thing with the second and third cards.

When you pick up the fourth card, tear it the same way. As you place each piece in the bag, bend them in half with your fingertips. (Do not go slow. Timing is important. Act smooth). Continue tearing the remaining cards, placing them in the bag, one piece at a time.

State that you will attempt the impossible. Place your hand inside the bag and feel for a bent card. As you pull it out of the bag, straighten it with your finger tips. Place it in your free hand, as you reach in to find another bent piece. (Do not lay the pieces on the table, as the bends may be noticeable.) As

Mr. Jim with teachers performing the Chinese Rings as part of his work in schools and classrooms.

you pull out the second piece, hold it up to the first piece. The spectator will realize that you have just pulled out two pieces of the same card!

Reach in again and locate another bent portion. Hold this piece next to the others. Another match! Do the same thing with the last piece.

Smile and then crumple the pieces before tossing them away. (This destroys the secret folds.)

THE PENETRATING RING

Materials

3-foot length of rope and a finger ring

Trick

A finger ring is threaded onto a rope, and held securely in your closed fist. The ends of the rope are criss-crossed and tied on the top of your hand. After your volunteer places her hand under yours, the ring suddenly, and magically, melts through the solid rope, falling into her hand!

Using sleight-of-hand (or hands in this case), the ring is secretly removed from the rope and held inside the fist until the trick's end.

Begin by threading the rope through the ring. Now hold the rope's ends with both hands so that the ring hangs down in the middle. Invite your volunteer to tug on the ring, confirming that it is

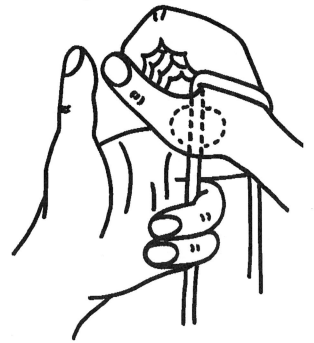

secure. Next, hold both ends in the left hand, while the open right hand drops down between the ends, resting upon the ring. Close the right hand around the ring. Lift the right hand, letting the ends drop.

While asking your volunteer if they are familiar with knots—and the questioning is creating mis-direction from your actions—your left hand takes the rope by the right thumb and, in one smooth motion, lifts the rope over the hand and down the other (little-finger) side of the right hand, next to the rope hanging there. The left hand should slide all the way down the rope.

Your left hand takes the rope that is hanging by the right little finger, as your right hand tilts to the right (thumb up, little finger down). Open the right hand's little fingers just enough to allow the ring to slide out and down the rope into the left little fingers. [See Figure 1.]

(Although the left hand provides coverage for the ring's transfer, continue your dialogue with the volunteer asking, "Do you know the difference between a 'granny' and 'bowline' knot?" Asking this forces her to think about your question, distracting her from your hand movements. Keep in mind, if you look at a person's eyes when talking to them, they will often look at yours, taking their eyes off your actions—misdirection.)

With the ring palmed, slide your left hand along the rope as you pull it up and over the right hand, and down the thumb side. When your hand reach-es the bottom, and slides off the rope, keep the ring finger- palmed. The left hand should hang lifeless, and unsuspecting, by your left side, while the right hand remains held out, with the two ropes criss-crossed over it. [See Figure 2.]

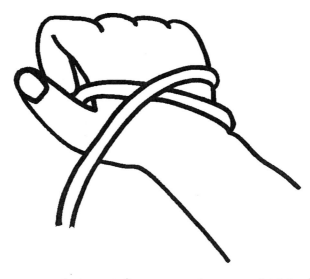

Lift your left hand (keeping the ring hidden), and lay your thumb on the back of the right hand, where the ropes criss-cross. While holding the rope down, have the volunteer tie the ends into a bow, like a shoelace. While they are doing this, your right fingers secretly take the ring from the left palm. When she is finished tying the bow, drop your left hand by your side.

Ask your volunteer to place her open hand palm up under your (palm down) right hand. Wave a wand over your hand and allow the ring to drop into her palm. You will probably see a surprised expression come over her face. Slowly turn your right hand over, opening it slowly. Slide the tied rope off with your left hand and lay it in hers. Everything can be examined.

ROPE THROUGH BODY

Materials
Two ropes, about five-feet long each

Trick

Two long ropes are wrapped around your back side, then criss-crossed over your stomach. Volunteers stand at your right and left sides, holding the ends of the ropes. Suddenly, the ropes are pulled tightly, and cut through your body!

This trick is described in Mark Wilson's Cyclopedia of Magic (p. 387-390). In his book, the rope is wrapped around the magician's thighs, while he is sitting. However, I prefer to perform this while standing. (A chair is not always available and a rope through a person's mid-section seems more dramatic, to me.)

Hold up two ropes, each about five feet in length. After you show both ropes to be solid and strong, invite two volunteers to assist you, by standing at your sides. While showing each assistant where to stand, fold the ropes in half, at their centers, forming a loop in each. Insert one loop through the other and pull it back about three inches. This will form a J hook. [See Figure 1.] The audience must not see this action.

Concealing the hooked loops in your left hand, move the ropes behind your back. Reach back with your right hand, grasping the two ends of the same rope, bringing them around to your right. Place the hooked portion of the rope against your back and pull the other two ends to your left.

(The tip of the hook should lie against your body. If you maintain pressure against the back, by continuously pulling on both ropes, the hook

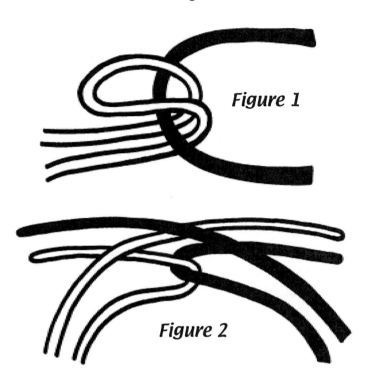

Figure 1

Figure 2

should not come apart. It is best to place the hook slightly off the back's center, since the small of the back curves inward. Maintain the pressure during the routine, or the ropes will come apart. If you try this around your thigh, you can see how the hook functions.)

Holding two ends in each hand, ask your volunteers to select one of the two ends, from their own side, and trade with the other volunteer, across the front of your body. Two, of the four ends, are now criss-crossed in front of you. [See Figure 2.] The crossed ends are placed back in your hands (along with the two ends that you have been continuously holding). You must maintain pressure on your back, and the hook, during this entire process.

After the ropes are crossed and tied, you could

have the volunteers slide a couple of bangles onto the rope's four ends, and close to your body. The rings give an added illusion of being securely bound.

Now remind the audience that you have wrapped two solid ropes around your body, and that your volunteers freely selected two of the ends to tie around you. The final step will be your attempt to break free of the solid ropes, by passing through them!

Begin to pull the ends tighter, particularly the two that have been criss-crossed in front. The audience will see these tightening into your stomach. Then, as you exhale (reducing your body size and creating slack in the rope) take a small, but forceful step forward with one foot, while yanking the rope's ends outward. (Play this up big!) The ropes will snap to your front-side, creating the illusion that the ropes just passed through your body!

I love this rope trick, and I use it in almost every show. The long ropes are very visual, causing the trick to appear larger than it is. Escapes are exciting, because they add an element of intensity or danger. (After all, isn't it characters like Superman that escape from impossible conditions?)

Of course, rope, like many other things, can be dangerous if misused. Always be careful when handling rope to make sure it is not wrapped around any part of your body where circulation can be cut off. If in doubt about the safety of any magic trick or stunt, always ask an adult about it first.

FORCED COLOR

Materials

Paper bag, paper and pen

Trick

You can predict any color!

Prepare by secretly writing the word green on the bottom of the lunch bag.

After tearing off pieces of paper, ask your volunteer to name some popular colors. Offer to write them down on separate pieces of paper. Be sure that the spectator can not see what you are writing on the pieces. Instead of writing the colors that he calls out, write the word green on every piece, tossing them into the bag. He will assume that you are writing the colors he names. Continue until he says "green." (You may have to offer some suggestions if he does not say it, but don't say it yourself!) Whey he says "green," act as if the pen is running out of ink, and lay it down. He should see the word green on the paper. (Seeing this, he will assume that you have been writing all the words.)

Throw the last piece of paper in the bag and ask the volunteer to shake it, mixing the pieces. Taking the bag back, hold it above his head and ask him to reach into the bag and pull out one piece.

Finally, state that you made a prediction earlier. Ask him to read the color's name (it will be green). Turn the bag over, and show him the word green on the bottom. (Don't let pieces fall out!) Crumple the bag and toss it away.

PRODUCTION SURPRISE

Materials

Shoe box with lid, thread, paper clip, and small object

Trick

You produce an object from an empty box!

Place the box so that one (wide) side is near you. Bend out one end of a paper clip and poke it through the back lip of the lid (not through the top). Now bend the clip's end so it will stay attached to the lid.

Tie one end of the thread to the clip. Tie the other end to the small object. The object should be small enough, and the thread short enough so that the object will hang behind the lid when the lifted, hidden from view.

When performing, lift the lid off the box from the back side, and tip the box forward, showing that it is empty. As you lower and replace the lid, the object will drop back into the box. When you are ready to reveal the object, lift the lid from the front. The object, or your fingers, can hide the thread from view, or detach the object from the thread before bringing it out.

PART 2 - CARD TRICKS

CARD BOX READING

Materials

Card deck and box

Trick

You can name any selected card!

Prepare by cutting a secret hole in the right bottom corner of the box, on the flap side. When the cards are inside the box, you can see the bottom card's suit and value through the hole.

Remove the cards from the box, explaining how you will attempt to read the spectator's mind. (Keep the hole hidden. If you put your finger over it, you can flash the backside of the box.) Spread the cards, asking the spectator to select one while you turn your head away. Ask him to lay his card on the table, and lay the face-down deck on it. In this way, you could not see the face or back of the chosen card.

Pick up the box, with the flap-side (hole) down, and slide the face-down deck inside. Close the flap. As you lift the box, glance at the hole, noting the card's value and suit. Look into the spectators eyes, and act as if you are getting an image of the card. Take your time, making your revelation more mysterious.

CRISS-CROSS FORCE

Materials

Deck of cards

Trick

Spectator freely chooses any card and you immediately state the card's name!

Get a peek of the bottom card; you can do this as you take the cards out of the box. Hold the face-down deck in your left hand. With your right hand over the deck, grasp the small ends of the deck with your thumb and middle finger.

Explain how you will riffle through the cards with your left thumb, stopping when he says "Stop." When he does, immediately lift the top portion of the deck with your right hand and place it on the table. Quickly place the bottom portion on what was the top portion, creating a criss-cross (+) pattern.

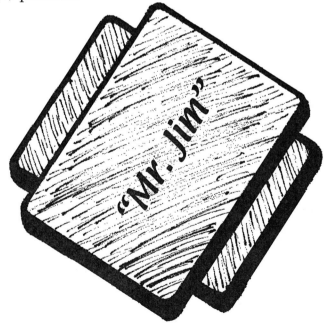

The spectator will assume that the deck was cut where they called "Stop." Actually, the bottom card (that you peeked at) is now the bottom card of the top portion.

Ask the spectator if they happen to know which card they cut to. They will probably say "No." (If they guess correctly, congratulate them on being a card predictor!) Act as if you are trying to get a picture of the card in your mind, and finish by stating the card's name. Turn over the top portion to reveal your amazing accuracy!

9 CARD PREDICTION

Materials

Any 9 cards and an assistant

Trick

You enter a room and immediately state which card was chosen.

Prepare by explaining to your assistant how you will lay out 9 cards, forming a square (three rows, with three cards in each row). After you leave the room, a volunteer will point to a card. When you return, your assistant will point to a card, asking you if it is the selection.

The first card that the assistant points to is the key to this trick. The assistant will touch the first card according to the location of the selected card. For example, if the spectator selected the upper-center card, then the assistant is to touch the upper-center portion of the first card. You now know which card was selected.

Say "no" to each card your assistant touches, until he touches the chosen card.

FAST HAND SLIDER

Materials

Any 5 playing cards and a paper clip

Trick

You can cause a paper clip to move to the exact card!

Let us assume that you are holding four Kings with an Ace in the middle. Hold the five cards face up, and spread them to the right (in a straight line; not in a fan). Each card should overlap half of the next one. Hold the cards firmly so they do not move.

Turn the cards face down, and invite the spectator to "clip the Ace in the middle." (Flipping the cards over creates an illusion. The middle card, from the back view, is actually the face card on the end, from the front view.)

After the (face down) card is clipped, explain how you will cause the clip to slide across the cards, stopping on the very last card. "Too much power," you say, "could cause the card to slide off completely."

The fact is, no skill is needed! Give your wrist a quick snap away from you, while turning your hand over. The cards will now be face up, and the clip will be found on the last card! Although the clip has not moved, you created the illusion that the clip slid across two cards, stopping on the last. Immediately remove the clip off and pocket it, saying "Whew! I almost lost the touch!"

Practice the movements and patter in front of the mirror.

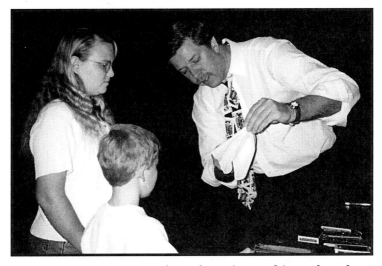

Mr. Jim's most amazing feat of magic: teaching others how to perform magic themselves!

ELMER - THE AMAZING FLEA!

Materials

Playing cards

Trick

A volunteer's card is lost in the deck. No problem! Your trained flea finds it!

A simple set-up is required. Lay the four Aces face down in a pile. Lay any 5-card face up on top of them. Place the remainder of the face-down deck on top of all five cards.

Spread the cards and ask your volunteer to select one, any one, remember it, and place it face down on top of the deck. (While spreading the cards, do not expose the face up 5-card, near the bottom of the deck.) Holding the deck in your left hand, have the volunteer cut off the upper half, complete the cut, and square the deck. The card is now lost somewhere in the middle of the deck.

Now, reach into a pocket and (pretend to) pro-

duce Elmer, your pet flea, placing him on top of the deck. Explain that Elmer will locate the volunteer's card, pull it out of the deck, flip it face-up, and slide it back in—quicker than the human eye can see! After Elmer has (apparently) performed this feat in your hand, spread the cards until you come to the face-up 5-card. Act excited about it! After all, you never saw their card, so you would assume that Elmer found the correct one. However, your excitement quickly fades as your volunteer points out that the 5-card is not her card.

Suddenly, you are interrupted by Elmer's call, a faint scream that only you can hear. Lifting him up to your ear, he whispers something important. "Oh," you say, "Elmer says he turned over the 'indicator' card." Explain that the indicator card indicates where the volunteer's card can be found. Count down five more cards, turning over the card. It is your volunteer's card! Elmer did it! But there is more. Slowly turn over the other cards, revealing the four Aces. "Elmer," you say, "wanted you to have a good hand to go with your card!"

LOCATE ANY CARD

Materials

Deck of cards

Trick

You can immediately locate a lost card!

Spread the cards and allow the spectator to take one, and show it to everyone. Place the deck on your left palm and lift up half of the cards with your right hand. Ask the spectator to lay his card face down on the bottom half. As he lays it down, keep a little break under his card with your left little-finger, and immediately lay the top portion (in your right hand) on his card. As you are doing this, put a little pressure on the corner of his card with your little finger, causing the right corner nearest you to crease upward. (The spectator can not see this, because your right hand covers this action).

Cut the deck a few times, losing the card in the deck. Next, spread the cards with the faces toward the spectator, explaining that you will use his eyes to identify his card. As you spread the cards, from one hand to the other, do not expose the bent corner. When you come to his card, lift it by the corner, revealing your abilities.

(As you return the card to the deck, bend the corner back into shape.)

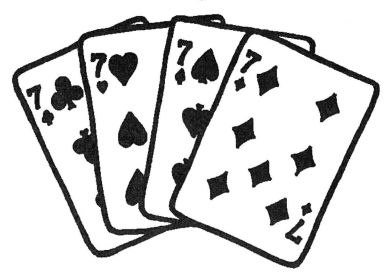

7-CARD PILE

Materials

Deck of cards, pencil, paper

Trick

You predict which pile the spectator will chose!

Prepare by placing all four 7's on the top of the deck, and return the cards to the box. Then write "You will choose the 7 pile" on a piece of paper, and put it away.

Begin by explaining that you can predict what cards a spectator will choose, before they know! Remove the deck from the box and deal four cards face down in a pile. (This pile contains the four 7's.) Next, count off seven cards into another pile. (Count to yourself. The spectator should not be aware of the actual number.)

Ask the spectator to choose either pile, and the other will be discarded into the (middle of) the deck. This action will remove the secret. Finally, reveal your written prediction.

Regardless which pile they choose, the prediction will be correct. One pile has seven cards and the other pile has all the 7's.

Too make the trick more convincing, close with one of these actions. If they choose the seven cards, pickup the other pile and count the four face down cards. If they choose the four 7's, turn the seven cards over showing a variety of cards.

REDS FROM NOWHERE!

Materials
Deck of cards
Trick
Two cards suddenly appear after they become lost in the deck!

Prepare by placing the 8-Diamonds, 9-Hearts and 8-hearts on the top of the deck, and the 9-Diamonds on the bottom of the deck. (The 8-hearts should be third from the top.) Return the cards to the card box.

(Note: the four selected cards are all red, and all four appear the same—the "8" and "9" cards look similar. This selection is intentional, as you will see below.)

Begin by removing the deck from the box. Slide off the top two cards (8-D and 9-H) and briefly turn them face-up stating, "We will use two cards for this trick." Immediately turn them face-down and insert them somewhere near the middle, in two different places. (You do not want the spectator to remember these cards. Keep the pattern and actions moving, distracting the volunteer's attention.)

Now ask, "Wouldn't it be neat if I could simply

toss the deck through the air and those two cards would suddenly appear?" While holding the deck face-down in the right-hand, gently squeeze the top and bottom cards, and give the deck a quick toss into the left hand. With the correct amount of pressure, the deck will fly into the left hand, leaving the top (8-H) and bottom (9-D) cards between the right finger tips. The motion is so quick that they will not know where the two cards came from. Turn the two cards face up and say, "All you need is a little magic!"

FLIPPED FAKE-OUT

Materials
Deck of cards
Trick
The spectator knows you are wrong. Or does he? Prepare by glimpsing the bottom card.

Ask the spectator to select any card from the deck, remember it, and lay it face-down on top of the deck. Give the cards a complete cut. (The bottom, or key, card is now on top of their card, somewhere near the middle of the deck.)

Explain that it would be too easy to locate their card, because you both know that it is near the middle of the deck. Ask the spectator to cut the deck five more times. (Most people assume that cutting the cards mixes them up. It does not. It only changes their order. In other words, your card will always be on top of their card, no matter how many times the deck is cut.)

Holding the deck face down, begin dealing one card at a time face up unto the table. As you deal, lay each card so it covers part of the card that was laid before it. In this way, you can still see a portion of the previous card. Deal the cards in a tight small circle.

Because the key card is above the selected card, you will see it first. Do not interrupt your dealing when you see your card. Rather, remember the next card that is dealt—this is his card. Deal a few more cards, and then stop.

Look up at the spectator and say, "I am confident that the next card I turn over will be your card!" Slide the top card on the deck slightly to the side, as if you are about to deal it. He will assume that you are wrong, because you already dealt their card. Regardless of his response, reach down and pick up his card, and turn it face-down.

RED AND BLACK SECRET

Materials

Deck of cards

Trick

You can find a spectator's card by her finger-prints!

Prepare the deck by separating the black cards (spades and clubs) from the red cards (hearts and diamonds). Place the black cards face down on top of the face down red cards. Return the cards to the box.

Removing the cards from the box, hold them face-down in your left hand. Begin spreading the top (black) cards to the right hand, asking the spectator to "select one card". Slowly spread the cards, as you want the spectator to select a black card from the top half. After she removes a card, ask her to remember it, and return it to the deck.

As you are speaking continue spreading the cards until you reach the bottom (red) section. Her black card will enter the red section of the deck. Close the spread and square the cards.

Ask her to cut the deck a few times. (She will wrongly assume that the cuts are mixing the cards. The order remains the same.)

Hold the cards up, facing you, and slowly spread them. The reds and blacks are still separated, but one black card will be found in the red section. This is the spectator's card. When you locate her card, pause and look at the fingerprints on her fingers. Then look back at the cards and say "This looks like your fingerprint on this card." Pull the card out and hand it to her.

(A riffle shuffle will mix the blacks and reds, destroying the secret.)

"DO AS I DO"

Materials

Deck of cards

Trick

The spectator unknowingly locates two previously selected cards!

Hand the deck to the spectator, and ask her to shuffle the cards. Lift up half of the cards, glimpsing the bottom card as you hand them to her. Take the bottom half for yourself.

Ask the spectator to remove any card from the center of her pack, as you do the same with yours. Ask her to remember her card, place it on top of her deck, and cut the deck, as you do the same with your pack. (You do not need to remember the card you selected. It is not used in this trick.) Her cut has placed your card (the bottom card that you glimpsed in her pile) on top of her selected card, and both are now in the middle of her pile.

Spread your cards face down and ask her to touch one. Remove this card, keeping it face down. Ask her to riffle down through her packet, stopping so you can insert the card. Ask her to cut the deck a couple times. (Cutting the packet twice will keep the two selected cards near the middle).

Comment on the "very slim chance" of her selecting your card, and placing it next to her card. State the name of the card you glimpsed at the beginning, while turning your pile face up. Spread your cards. Then exclaim, "My card is not here!"

Ask her to turn her cards face up and spread them, as she states the name of her card. Amazingly, your card is found next to hers!

(Note: if the card from your pack is placed between the two selected cards, comment on the near perfect coincidence of her actions.)

ESP?

Materials
Deck of cards, index card and envelope
Trick
You can predict which card the spectator will choose, regardless of his choices!

Prepare by secretly placing two selected cards on top of the deck. Write the names of the cards on an index card; one name on each side. Place the prediction in an envelope.

Lay the envelope in view, and begin dealing the cards onto the table, one on top of the other. (The two on the bottom are the selected cards.) After you have dealt about ten cards, invite the volunteer to say "Stop" at any time. When he does, place the cards that are still in your hand back in the box.

Pick up the pile on the table. Begin dealing the cards into two piles, alternating back-and-forth. (When finished, the top two cards will be the selected cards.

Point out that no one could have known how many cards, or even which cards, were going to be part of the original pile, since the volunteer could freely say "Stop." Nor could anyone know in advance which cards would be in which pile. And, "no one could possibly know which of the two piles the spectator is now going to choose." Ask him to select one, and discard the other.

Remove the top card and lay it aside. Turn the remaining cards face up, stating that "any of these cards could have been the top card, but you decided when and where to stop, while I was dealing." Place the cards in the box, leaving only one card on the table.

Turn the card face-up, and pause for a moment. Now pick up the envelope and tear across the end, to open it. Look down inside, noting which way the card is turned. Hold the envelope so the correct card name is face up as you bring it out.

Throw away the card and envelope. You don't want them to see the other side of the index card.

motion is smooth,
ng the same spot

en practicing with
wo balls. (Remem-
well, you certainly
his point, I explain
he balls are part of
reduce the number

e my students toss
let the floor catch
; helps you focus on
. If you can't throw
second, if the balls
your shoulders, the
ur feet. If they are
rection!—then you
narks.)

, you will toss one,
tossing the ball in
houlder. As the ball
ll in the left hand
left hand will catch
ht hand. Next time
When juggling, it is
y with both hands.
iand, or arm, to do

ed to toss and catch
ke it easier for your
tly above head level.

ontinue to throw the
ime, your hands will

PART 3 - JUGGLING

Many magicians are jugglers. Consequently, our magic camps include juggling, and so does this book. Juggling is great because once you know how, you can juggle anytime, anywhere, with almost anything. Juggling is also good exercise, for the body and the brain! And juggling also reinforces many important life lessons.

Kent Cummins (director of the Austin, Texas Magic Camp) is a professional juggler, and started me in juggling. Kent pointed out that many people never follow through with juggling because they feel like a failure when they drop the balls. The truth is, if we drop the balls, we are probably getting better!

Obviously, none of us are going to become professional jugglers the first time we toss three balls in the air. But every time you toss them up correctly, you are practicing. And practice will lead to success. Thus, dropping is part of growing! (And don't forget: if you drop the ball, the floor will catch it for you!)

If you do not have any juggling balls, and would like to learn about juggling without spending money, you could use "hacky sack" balls, fill some old socks with dry beans (like bean bags), or just ball up some gym socks.

The pattern that we will learn first is called the "3-ball Cascade." (The ball moves in a path that looks like a horizontal figure-8. Most children

Teaching a physical education teacher the skills of juggling.

learn the "shower" movement, which is created by tossing the ball over the head in an arch, creating a circular pattern.) To see the cascade pattern in slow motion, begin with one ball in your right hand, at your lower right side. Now move the ball upward and left to your left shoulder. Lower the ball down your left side, then upward toward your

for now, making sure that natural, and consistent, above the shoulder every

Assuming that you hav one ball, you will now atter ber, if you can not toss one can not toss two balls well! to my students that droppi learning, and only practice of drops.

(The truth is, I usually the balls in the air, and t them. Why? First, because throwing rather than catch well, you won't catch well. are hitting the "marks" abc balls should land in front c landing far away—in any need to work on hitting you

With one ball in each ha and then the other. Begin the right hand above the le reaches its peak, toss the above the right shoulder. T its ball first, and then the begin with your left hand. best to practice every acti Don't allow your "favorite' more than the other.)

While you must be prepa the balls quickly, you will n self if you toss the balls slig This will give you extra tim

But remember this, if you balls in the same place every

soon know where they must be to catch the balls.

Above all, don't give up! Keep trying! Practice! You can do it!

Three balls are more challenging than two, just as two are more challenging than one. But you have done two, and you can do three! Begin by holding two balls in, let us say, the right hand, and one ball in the left. The hand with two balls begins—that is, your right hand. You will toss and release one of the two balls in your right hand. Then you will toss the ball in your left hand. Finally, you will toss the last ball, in your right hand.

In other words, it looks like this: right-left-right or left-right-left.

Are you nervous about catching all three balls? Don't be! Remember your "friend," the floor? Use the floor at the beginning. Focus on hitting your marks. Focus on tossing each ball above your head, for that needed height. Again, throwing is more important than catching!

Okay, here is your last assignment. No, not four balls. Well, sort of four. Let me explain. We will only use three balls. However, we will try a fourth throw—four balls in the air, if you will.

This time, you only need to catch the first ball (of the three) and toss it back up. For example, if you catch the first ball in the left hand, then toss it back up toward the right shoulder. That's it! That's all! Just catch the first ball and toss it back up at your mark. Soon, perhaps very soon, you will be able to catch a second ball out of the air and toss it back up. That will make throw number five. Then six, seven, eight—well, you get the picture.

But don't quit at three-ball juggling! Try out a few other types.

You could juggle in columns, instead of a fig-ure-8. Now, the balls are tossed straight up, and fall straight down. You can hold two balls in one hand, or three balls in two hands. While one (or two) is going up, one (or two) is coming down. They look like two elevators passing each other: one going up and the other coming down. Each ball must go up and down in the same place, as if there was an invisible track in the air.

To perform a one-handed column, hold two balls, side-by-side in your right hand, in front of you. Toss the left ball straight up. As it reaches its peak, move your hand slightly to the right and quickly toss up the other one. The left ball will come down as the right one is going up. As the right ball reaches its peak, the left ball should be landing in your hand. Quickly toss the ball back up, and get ready to catch the other.

PART 4 - CUP STACKING

If you think juggling is cool, you'll love cup stacking—or so says Miss Sara! Now don't get me wrong. I love juggling. But cup stacking is like a super simple way to juggle, at a fast and wild pace! The basic idea behind cup stacking is that you have to stack ("up stack") and unstack ("down stack") twelve mouth-down specially designed plastic cups* into various sized pyramids, at lightning speed!

You can compete against yourself, for your fastest time, against others, with a partner, as teams, and more. And, while you're having fun, you are actually developing personal skills, like hand-eye coordination, right and left hand dexterity (its called, ambidexterity), and better concentration. That may sound like a lot of work, but its not.

You begin by up stacking 3 mouth-down cups, into a small pyramid, and immediately taking them back down. Next, you build a 3-3; build the first pyramid, then the second one, return to the first one and take it down, and then take down

Cup-stacking fun! Sara (below) instructing.

Sara gets cup-stacking tips from current world champion, Emily Fox.

the second one. Pretty simple, huh? Finally, you do a series called the 3-3-3. Begin by up stacking at either end, then the middle stack, and finally the other end. Again, return to the first stack and down stack it, then the middle, then the last stack. In other words, you take down the stacks in the same order that you put them up.

Care for a bigger challenge? Try a six stack! One way to stack this pyramid (3 on the bottom, 2 in the middle, and 1 on top) is to begin with all six cups down stacked. Then lift one cup in each hand, and begin up stacking your pyramid. I refer to this as the "2-2-2" method, and it is pretty simple.

A quicker way to up stack the six, and almost

as easy, is called the "3-2-1" method. You begin by picking up three cups together with one hand, and two more with the other hand. (You now have the cups divided into 3-2-1. I told you it was easy!) Using the cup on the table as the center bottom cup for your pyramid, bring down the hand with the three-cups, dropping one from the bottom, next to the center cup. Now bring down the other hand (that has two cups) on the other side of the center cup and release a cup from the bottom. Now you have 3 cups—your foundation—on the table. Keep alternating your hands, back and forth, till you reach the top. That's it! That is how professional cup stackers do it! It's the fastest way to up stack a six-stack—assuming that you practice.

Ready for the "big time?" Lay your cups out in the following order: 3-6-3. This is what you would see at a cup stacking competition (www.worldcupstackingassociation.org). You would also see stackers performing the Cycle, which begins with the 3-6-3, then a 6-6, then a 1-10-1, ending back in a down stacked 3-6-3! (When building a 1-10-1 stack, two cups must be placed on the table, one up and one down, on each side of the pyramid.)

Can you use any plastic or paper cup for cup stacking? Yes, but the results won't be the same. That is why specially designed cups are made for this sport. Be sure to check the resource page at the end of the book for more information on cup stacking and supplies.

* Speed Stacks (www.speedstacks.com)

PART 5 -
BALLOON SCULPTING

I took up balloon sculpting since I perform restaurant magic. I found that children, their parents, and even grandparents, love to watch a balloon being sculptured into an animal or other object. In fact, many people assume that a magician can make a balloon animal. Regardless, I have enjoyed balloon sculpting. The easiest of my creations are appreciated by the spectators, and the harder ones give me a personal challenge.

I have provided the basic instructions below for making a simple mouse and a dog-shaped balloon. If you can make a mouse, you can make a dog. If you can make a dog, you can make a giraffe. From there, you can make a zoo of balloon animals!

I use balloons called a "2-60." The balloons are 2-inches wide by 60-inches long. Large department stores, party stores or magic shops carry these. (You can also order the balloons through websites. See the resource list at the end of this book.) Many balloon packages will come with a hand air-pump. You can also use a basketball pump, if it has a tapered plastic needle.

To create a mouse, fill about 12-inches of the balloon with air. Hold the "nose," or knotted end, in your left hand (hand on top of the balloon), with the nose to the left and the tail to the right. The left hand never twists; it remains still, holding the balloon.

Keeping in mind that you will be making four bubbles, hold your right hand over the balloon and pinch it about 3-inches from the knot, with your right thumb and first (index) finger. Now twist your right hand (top of the hand away from you) about three times, forming your first bubble—this will be the mouse's head. (Always twist your right hand in the same direction, or your bubbles may come apart.)

As your left hand continues to hold the "head," slide the balloon to the left, inside your left hand, so your left thumb and first finger can grasp the

Kristi and Sara sculpting balloons at the county fair.

next bubble. The left hand must hold all the bubbles, or your bubbles will come undone. Make the next three bubbles in the same way as the first.

To complete the mouse, twist the two (you should have four) center bubbles together as one, three times, forming the ears. You now have a mouse!

But this is no ordinary mouse. It's a flying mouse! Form a circle with your thumb and first finger, and then close it a little. Drop the mouse's tail down through the hole, so its body is sitting on the circle. Grasp the tail with the other hand, pull down a little, and then release. It flies!

Are you ready to make a dog?

If you turn the mouse upside down, you will see what a dog's legs look like. That is because ears and legs are made the same way. In other words, you already know how to make a dog!

Fill all but 6 inches of the balloon with air and tie a knot. I always recommend squeezing the balloon gently with both hands (near the knotted end), pushing the air toward the tail. This softens the balloon, so it is not so tight, and less likely to pop while you are twisting it. (I always take this precaution when working in a restaurant.)

Now, follow these directions closely. Hold the balloon in your left hand so that the tied end is to your left and the tail (unfilled end) is to your right—just like you held the mouse. (Remember, your left hand will hold the balloon's bubbles while your right hand performs the pinch and twist.)

To make the dog's head, pinch-off a 2-inch bubble with your right fingers and twist a few times. Slide the bubble to the left, inside the left hand. Holding the bubble (the head) inside the hand, grasp the remainder of the balloon with your left fingers.

Now we will make the ears, just as we did with the mouse. While holding the head, pinch a smaller bubble (1-inch) with your right hand and twist. This is the first ear. Slide the balloon further to the left, holding both bubbles with the left hand. Pinch-off and twist another 1-inch bubble. You now have three bubbles: a head and two smaller ears. Now, carefully bend the head bubble down and beside the body of the balloon; the two ear bubbles will be sticking up. Grasp the ears with your right hand, and gently twist them three times. The head and ears are complete, and should not come apart.

We will make the neck and two front legs the same way as the head and ears. It is just that easy!

Hold the neck area with your left hand, and pinch-off and twist a 2-inch bubble with the right fingers. Slide the neck section into the left hand

and hold the remaining body with the left fingers.

To make the first front leg, pinch off a 3-inch bubble and twist (with the right fingers, of course). Hold on to all the bubbles with the left hand. Now pinch-off another 3-inch bubble and twist. Bend the balloon in half so the neck is beside the body, and the legs are on top. Holding the head and body portions together, grasp and twist both legs.

To create the back legs, repeat the previous steps. Instead of holding the neck section, hold the dog's belly in your left hand. Create the two bubbles for the back legs, leaving a small bubble for the dog's behind. The unfilled portion of the balloon is the tail.

RESOURCES

Books

Balloon Magic, Marvin L. Hardy; Pioneer (ISBN 0-9616600-1-5).

Magic With Cards, Frank Garcia and George Schindler, Barnes and Noble (ISBN 0-7607-1010-4).

Magic With Everyday Objects, George Schindler; Madison Books (ISBN 0-8128-2103-4).

Mark Wilson's Cyclopedia of Magic, Mark Wilson; Running Press (ISBN 1-56138-613-8).

Self-Working Table Magic, Karl Fulves; Dover (ISBN 0-486-24116-5).

The Complete Juggler, Dave Finnigan; Jugglebug (ISBN 0-9615521-0-7).

The Magic Handbook, Peter Eldin; Simon and Schuster (ISBN 0-671-55039-X).

Ventriloquism, George Schindler; Show-Biz Services (ISBN0-679-21025-3).

Also, don't forget 793.8 Dewy Decimal Number at your library where you'll find more books on how to do magic tricks.

Internet Resources

www.juggle.org – International Juggler's Association.

www.speedstacks.com – Cups, videos, and other supplies.

funfx.com – Pumps, balloons, and other supplies.

www.mr-jim.com – The latest news and information from Mr. Jim.

Organizations and Magazines

You may want to consider some of the monthly magazine publications that are also available, such as *MAGIC* (www.magicmagazine.com) or Genii (www.geniimagazine.com) magazines. You could also receive *M.U.M.* or *The Linking Ring*, byproducts of two magic organizations—Society of American Magicians (*www.magicsam.com*) and the International Brotherhood of Magicians (*www.magician.org*), respectively.

Mr. Jim's
MAGIC CAMP

The student named above has become familiar with a variety of magic—rope, card, coin, sleight, prediction. The signature above reflects his/her commitment to support the art of magic by promoting it through ongoing practice, following its rules, maintaining its secrets, and respecting the accomplishments of other magicians.

—"Mr. Jim" Merrills

After mastering the magic in this book, you will deserve this official recognition of your achievements. Please fill in your name and take pride in your accomplishment!